MW00436949

GAME
CHANGER

GAME
CHANGER

THIS JOURNAL BELONGS TO

## COMPETITOR'S CREED

I am a Christian first and last.
I am created in the likeness of God Almighty to bring Him glory.
I am a member of Team Jesus Christ.
I wear the colors of the cross.
I am a Competitor now and forever. I am made to strive, to strain,
to stretch and to succeed in the arena of competition.
I am a Christian competitor and as such,
I face my challenger with the face of Christ.
I do not trust in myself. I do not boast in my abilities
or believe in my own strength. I rely solely on the power of God.
I compete for the pleasure of my Heavenly Father,
the honor of Christ, and the reputation of the Holy Spirit.
My attitude on and off the field is above reproach—
my conduct beyond criticism.
Whether I am preparing, practicing or playing,
I submit to God's authority and those He has put over me.
I respect my coaches, officials, teammates and competitors
out of respect for the Lord.
My body is the temple of Jesus Christ.
I protect it from within and without.
Nothing enters my body that does not honor the Living God.
My sweat is an offering to my Master.
My soreness is a sacrifice to my Savior.
I give my all—all of the time. I do not give up. I do not give in.
I do not give out. I am the Lord's warrior—
a competitor by conviction and a disciple of determination.
I am confident beyond reason because
my confidence lies in Christ.
The results of my efforts must result in His glory.
Let the competition begin. Let the glory be God's.

# GAME CHANGER™

Make a play.
Acts 2:36

THE ATHLETE'S JOURNAL

**Now everyone who competes exercises self-control in everything. However, they do it to receive a perishable crown, but we an imperishable one. Therefore I do not run like one who runs aimlessly, or box like one who beats the air. Instead, I discipline my body and bring it under strict control, so that after preaching to others, I myself will not be disqualified.** — 1 Corinthians 9:25–27

**From God's perspective, the ultimate gamechanging play takes place when we make a radical change of direction by turning away from a life of sin and turning toward a relationship with His Son, Jesus Christ.**

**Let us lay aside every weight and the sin that so easily ensnares us, and run with endurance the race that lies before us, keeping our eyes on Jesus, the source and perfecter of our faith.** — Hebrews 12:1–2

**One thing that tends to get our attention as athletes is when the coach calls us out for not giving our best effort in practice, for an attitude issue, or for breaking a team rule. Has God ever called you out for something, or is He calling you out now?**

**Search me, God, and know my heart; test me and know my concerns. See if there is any offensive way in me; lead me in the everlasting way.**
— Psalm 139:23–24

For all of us, God is calling us to repentance. That is the act of turning away from sinful and selfish behavior and walking with Him toward a life of righteousness and selflessness. God is calling you to take the first step to becoming a gamechanger.

## TAYLOR-MADE: VIRGINIA TECH QB TYROD TAYLOR

BY CLAY MEYER

EVERY LEGITIMATE COLLEGE FOOTBALL TEAM HAS ONE. A FIELD GENERAL WHO KNOWS NO FEAR. A SIGNAL-CALLER WITH ICE IN HIS VEINS. SIMPLY STATED, A QUARTERBACK WHO CAN BOTH LEAD THE TEAM TO VICTORY AND PICK THEM UP IN DEFEAT.

Virginia Tech Quarterbacks Coach Mike O'Cain knows a great quarterback when he sees one. He has offered his instruction to plenty of them in his time, always reminding them of the reality of their position.

In light of the circumstances, O'Cain and the Hokies know they are blessed with Tyrod Taylor, the senior quarterback who has filled the position for the past four years.

"Tyrod is a natural leader because he is strong and demands respect, but not in a forceful way," O'Cain said. "He has that God-given ability to lead and is just a good guy to be around. The game is very important to him, but doing things the right way is even more important to him. He's put his life and his talents in God's hands."

The quarterback's stats have put him at the top of nearly every Virginia Tech record category and have earned him offensive MVP awards and ACC Championships. But Taylor doesn't want to be defined as "just" a quarterback. Unlike many of his position

counterparts across the country, Taylor seeks to remain humble and unassuming—a man who isn't awash in all he can do, but in what he can't do on his own.

"Without God I can't do anything," Taylor said. "I have put my faith in Him, and through Him I believe I can achieve anything."

**TAYLOR'S MOST PRIZED POSSESSION THROUGH IT ALL HAS REMAINED HIS RELATIONSHIP WITH THE LORD, WHICH HAS DEEPENED SIGNIFICANTLY SINCE HIS DECISION TO FOLLOW HIM YEARS AGO.**

"A lot of people back home are looking up to me," he said. "It's crazy to think that I am so young but am still seen as a role model. I know there are a lot of eyes on me at all times, so I have to make sure I do the right thing and take that into consideration."

From FCA's *Sharing the Victory* magazine

**For God loved the world in this way: He gave His One and Only Son, so that everyone who believes in Him will not perish but have eternal life.**
— John 3:16

**Jesus became the ultimate Gamechanger when He died on the cross in order to pay for our sin. Before we can become a gamechanger for Him, we must first recognize our need for salvation through the blood of Christ.**

**My soul finds rest in God alone; my salvation comes from him. He alone is my rock and my salvation; he is my fortress, I will never be shaken.**
— Psalm 62:1–2 NIV

**Ask God to reveal those areas in your life that need a change of direction, including those you might not be aware of. Ask for guidance from His Spirit to help you become the gamechanger that He desires you to be.**

**God, create a clean heart for me and renew a steadfast spirit within me.**
— Psalm 51:10

Spiritual disciplines must become a high priority and should be practiced daily. We need to have the proper stance before God—a stance that is based upon humility and a holy fear (respect and reverence) for His glory and power. In other words, we must surrender to God and His will for our lives.

**Therefore, get your minds ready for action, being self-disciplined, and set your hope completely on the grace to be brought to you at the revelation of Jesus Christ.... Do not be conformed to the desires of your former ignorance but, as the One who called you is holy, you also are to be holy in all your conduct.** — 1 Peter 1:13–15

## THE HEART OF TEXAS
BY CLAY MEYER

FROM THE TIME COLT MCCOY STARTED PLAYING FOOTBALL, PEOPLE KNEW HE WAS GOING TO BE SPECIAL.

"A guy told me after the third game Colt played as a seventh grader that he was going to win the Heisman one day," said his dad, Brad McCoy. "I just laughed and told him he was crazy. But it was obviously noticeable that he had a lot of special characteristics."

At the time, McCoy was developing in more ways than on the football field. He also was cultivating a close relationship with the Lord. At age 14, McCoy gave his life to Christ and was baptized shortly after.

Almost simultaneously, both McCoy's spiritual and football development shifted into overdrive. He had been involved with FCA since middle school, but with a new faith commitment, the Huddle meetings and church services took on new meaning. Godly leadership began to determine his actions.

Back on the field McCoy's football fame skyrocketed. His stats drew prominent coaches from around the country to the Texas plains and into the McCoys' living room. But McCoy was a Texas Longhorn through and through, and he committed to proudly donning the signature burnt orange.

Redshirted in his first year at UT, McCoy ran the Longhorns' scout-team offense in practice, eventually aiding in their 2005 BCS National Championship victory. Two days after a come-from-behind victory over USC, McCoy received a text message from quarterback Vince Young saying that he would forego his senior year and enter the NFL draft. The boy from Tuscola would now have some large shoes to fill in taking over one of the most highly scrutinized positions in the country: the starting quarterback of the Texas Longhorns.

**MCCOY RECOGNIZED THE PROMOTION AS AN OPPORTUNITY TO GLORIFY GOD AND HAS MAINTAINED THAT HUMBLE MINDSET IN THE FOUR YEARS OF SUCCESS THAT HAVE FOLLOWED.**

"I can prepare and practice as much as I want, but in the end I have to trust God with the results," he said. "It's not about me and never has been. It's not about what I do or what I say; it's about living for Christ and accomplishing His will for my life."

From FCA's *Sharing the Victory* magazine

When it comes to the Christian walk, our stance before God is important We don't just wake up one morning and suddenly become spiritual giants. It takes a daily commitment to key disciplines and a right attitude toward God to successfully fulfill His plan for our lives and become a gamechanger for Him.

**One thing I do: Forgetting what is behind and straining toward what is ahead, I press on toward the goal to win the prize for which God has called me heavenward in Christ Jesus.** — Philippians 3:13–14 NIV

**Unfortunately in today's sports environment, a humble stance is often replaced with pride and arrogance. Yet some of the most fulfilling moments in athletics take place when players put others first for a greater cause.**

**"Humble yourselves before the Lord, and He will exalt you" (James 4:10). What are some ways you can humble yourself as an athlete and how might this Scripture play out when that happens?**

**Beyond humility, we must also have a "holy fear" of God. This doesn't mean we are afraid of displeasing Him and experiencing His wrath or anger. Instead, we should have a stance of respect and reverence. We should be in awe of His power and seek out ways that we can please Him and fulfill His expectations for our lives.**

**How happy is everyone who fears the LORD, who walks in His ways! You will surely eat what your hands have worked for. You will be happy, and it will go well for you.** — Psalm 128:1–2

**As we solidify our stance, God will put us in a position to bring glory to Him—through our athletic skills, through our relationships, through the way we handle adversity, and through the way He blesses us and supplies our needs.**

## D-NASTY SUNSHINE
BY CHAD BONHAM

WHEN THE LOS ANGELES SPARKS NEED SOME DEFENSIVE INTENSITY AND FIERCE, SCRAPPY PLAY, THEY CALL ON THEIR INTIMIDATOR, "D-NASTY." BUT IF THEY'RE LOOKING FOR ENCOURAGEMENT AND A CHEERFUL RALLYING CRY, THEY TURN TO THE TEAMMATE THEY AFFECTIONATELY REFER TO AS "SUNSHINE."

Fortunately for L.A.'s front office, the Sparks don't have to waste two roster spots to fill both roles. D-Nasty and Sunshine are the same person: DeLisha Milton-Jones.

"On the court, I'm going to use every inch or every margin I can within the rules of the game to my advantage," she said. "I'm willing to do whatever it takes to win out there, but, if you look at my life, I try to be kind and help people. I just want people to be happy and enjoy life."

Milton-Jones admits that she once struggled to balance her passionate desire to aggressively mix it up on the court without damaging the integrity of her Christian witness.

"It really did bother me when people would view me as a dirty player when I was just being competitive," Milton-Jones said. "If I wasn't being competitive, I felt like I was getting punked out there

on the court. So, I had to ask myself the question of how to be competitive without losing my godliness."

It was a question that took time to answer. But, over the years, Milton-Jones has finally come to a point of peace regarding her competitive side.

**"I DISCOVERED THAT, THROUGH HIS SPIRIT, YOU CAN PUT A HARNESS ON THE COMPETITIVENESS AND CONTROL IT," SHE SAID. "YOU CAN GO OUT THERE AND PUSH AND SHOVE WITH THE BEST OF THEM AS LONG AS IT DOESN'T TAKE YOU TO THE POINT OF THINKING OR SAYING UNGODLY THINGS AND TAKING UNGODLY ACTIONS."**

"It's OK to be a radical for Christ," she says. "It's OK to stand up and be heard and not be shy about being a Christian. You don't have to be boastful or get in people's faces. It's about being confident and knowing that, at the end of the day, no matter what happens, you're taken care of. You're covered by the Lord."

From FCA's *Sharing the Victory* magazine

**You are the light of the world. A city situated on a hill cannot be hidden. No one lights a lamp and puts it under a basket, but rather on a lampstand, and it gives light for all who are in the house. In the same way, let your light shine before men, so that they may see your good works and give glory to your Father in heaven.** — Matthew 5:14–16

**Just as an athlete prepares for competition, as followers of Christ we must also be ready for the challenges and temptations that confront us every day. How do you think you might prepare yourself to face life's challenges as a Christian in today's world?**

BLAH BLAH BLAH
BLAH

**No temptation has overtaken you except what is common to humanity. God is faithful and He will not allow you to be tempted beyond what you are able, but with the temptation He will also provide a way of escape, so that you are able to bear it.** — 1 Corinthians 10:13

**Once you allow God to come into your life, He always has a plan for your life. He stands faithful if you trust Him. He is always there for you, no matter what you go through.** — Josh Hamilton

**"For I know the plans I have for you," declares the LORD, "plans to prosper you and not to harm you, plans to give you hope and a future."**
— Jeremiah 29:11 NIV

**The difference between champions and near champions is the ability to play for something outside of self.** — Lou Holtz, Hall of Fame football coach

# TRUE SAINT
BY JILL EWERT

IN 2005 SAN DIEGO CHARGERS QUARTERBACK DREW BREES HIT A CAREER-ALTERING SNAG IN THE LAST GAME OF THE SEASON WHEN A TACKLE INJURED HIS THROWING SHOULDER. ALREADY ON UNCERTAIN TERMS WITH THE CHARGERS, THE INJURY PUT A DAGGER IN HIS TIME WITH SAN DIEGO AND SENT BREES LOOKING FOR A NEW TEAM.

"At the time, I felt like that was the worst thing that could ever happen to me at the worst time," Brees said of the injury. "But, as I look back now, I can say, 'God, that was probably the best thing that could ever have happened to me.'"

In the wake of Hurricane Katrina, the New Orleans Saints organization found itself in complete chaos. With Brees on the market, the desperate Saints saw a chance to perhaps gain a powerful leader who could resuscitate the flatlining team. After a half-hearted contest from the Miami Dolphins, the Saints got their man.

Soon Brees and his wife, Brittany, found themselves relocating from sunny Southern California into the wreckage of New Orleans.

"At the time, we were all in the process of rebuilding," Brees said. "The Saints were trying to rebuild. The city was trying to rebuild. And I was trying to rebuild, literally, a shoulder and a career."

The Breeses purchased a home in New Orleans and made a complete move, committing wholeheartedly not only to the Saints but to the entire city.

On September 26, 2006, Saints fans returned to their home stadium to watch their team defeat the Atlanta Falcons. After the abysmal record of the previous season, the turnaround was stunning.

**LESS THAN TWO YEARS AFTER MAJOR DISASTER, THE SAINTS WERE BACK, AND NEW ORLEANS WAS RETURNING TO LIFE. AND IT APPEARED TO BE CONNECTED TO THE ACTIONS AND INSPIRATION OF LOUISIANA'S NEW HERO, DREW BREES.**

He's taught a team what it means to win, a city what it means to hope, and athletes worldwide what it means to persevere. As a result, Brees's new city has dubbed him their personal saint.

Brees rolls his eyes at the reference, knowing he's just doing what he knows to do: serve the Lord and love others.

From FCA's *Sharing the Victory* magazine

**Do nothing out of selfish ambition or vain conceit, but in humility consider others better than yourselves. Each of you should look not only to your own interests, but also to the interests of others.** — Philippians 2:3–4 NIV

**As believers we can't win in the game of life doing things on our own. We must be a part of a gamechanging team if we ever hope to truly fulfill God's plan.**

**Two are better than one because they have a good reward for their efforts. For if either falls, his companion can lift him up; but pity the one who falls without another to lift him up.** — Ecclesiastes 4:9–10

For some, the most important decisions don't happen on the field. They take place as we choose those people who will be a part of our *inner circle*—our closest group of friends. Being surrounded with the wrong teammates in our personal lives can too often result in a negative gamechanging play.

**Do not be deceived: “Bad company corrupts good morals.”**
— 1 Corinthians 15:33

**Can you think of examples of athletes—whether high profile or just people you know—who have squandered their talents and abilities because they surrounded themselves with the wrong "teammates"? What are some ways that having the wrong inner circle can cause you problems off the field?**

**If sinners entice you, don't be persuaded.... Don't travel that road with them or set foot on their path.** — Proverbs 1:10, 15

## THE CAMP EXPERIENCE
BY LIBBY PEIGEN,
OOLETWAH HIGH SCHOOL (TENN.)

I HAD NEVER EVEN READ A BIBLE. I DIDN'T UNDERSTAND WHAT SCRIPTURE WAS, AND I DIDN'T KNOW HOW TO DECIPHER ONE THING FROM ANOTHER IN IT. CHRISTIANITY JUST WASN'T IN MY LIFE.

In 2007, during my sophomore year, FCA's Julie Watson approached me at our state volleyball tournament and asked me if I wanted to get involved with FCA. I was obviously a bit confused as to why she would be asking me, but I knew there were two girls on my volleyball team who were really involved with it. I ended up going just for fun and to hang out with friends. That was a start, and, from there, Julie started encouraging me to go to an upcoming FCA Camp. Reluctantly, I agreed to go.

On the way there, I was dreading the whole thing. I was convinced that it was going to be stupid. And honestly, those feelings continued through the first days of camp. The people were all great, but I just felt like I shouldn't be there. Then we went on a prayer walk. Each girl in our Huddle was taking the opportunity to pray and tell her favorite Scripture, and all I could do was cry. I was so emotional thinking that I couldn't pray or do any of those things.

Later that night at worship, through the direction of my Huddle Leader and the camp staff, I finally realized all the grief and crying was like a rebirth within me. I gave my life to Christ that night in front of the whole camp in a flood of emotion and peace I'd never felt before.

**THE REST OF CAMP WAS AMAZING AS I FELT EMBRACED BY THE LORD AND ALL OF THE NEW FRIENDS I HAD MADE.**

Back at school, I'm now the president of our FCA, and we are so blessed to be able to make a difference on our campus. Julie Watson is also leading a Bible study with our volleyball girls, and we pray with the team before meals and games. I just love FCA because, without it, I wouldn't be walking with Christ like I am today. Thank God for FCA Camp!

From FCA's *Sharing the Victory* magazine

Becoming a gamechanger requires a series of gamechanging decisions. When it comes to the team concept, that decision takes place the moment you decide to surround yourself with a group of people who share common values, beliefs, and goals.

**A righteous man is cautious in friendship, but the way of the wicked leads them astray.** — Proverbs 12:26 NIV

**In ancient times, Shadrach, Meshach, and Abednego took a stand for God when they refused to bow to a golden idol, knowing they'd be thrown into a fiery furnace (Daniel 3). What character traits do you think these friends possessed that helped them stand up for their beliefs?**

**My eyes will be on the faithful in the land, that they may dwell with me.... No one who practices deceit will dwell in my house; no one who speaks falsely will stand in my presence.** — Psalm 101:6–7 NIV

**List some challenging situations or temptations that you are facing. How might having teammates like Shadrach, Meshach, and Abednego help you better overcome them?**

**Do not be mismatched with unbelievers. For what partnership is there between righteousness and lawlessness? Or what fellowship does light have with darkness?** — 2 Corinthians 6:14

**Begin thinking about people from whom you need to distance yourself. Ask God to help you gracefully and respectfully move apart from those friends, while still allowing you to influence them in a positive way for His glory.**

BLAH

# LIGHT IT UP
BY JILL EWERT

WHILE IT IS A PLUS FOR ANY TEAM TO GEL OFF THE FIELD, IT ALSO IS ONE OF THE MAIN REASONS WHY LIVING A GODLY LIFESTYLE IN THE LOCKER ROOM CAN BE A CHALLENGE. THE DESIRE TO CONNECT AS A TEAM IS A GOOD THING, BUT IT OFTEN BECOMES AN EXCUSE FOR COMPROMISING BEHAVIOR.

"When we struggle with whether we should fit in or honor God, we're basically saying who is more important to us," said Brian Roberts of the Baltimore Orioles. "Is it more important that these people like me, or is it more important that God looks at me and says, 'Well done, my good and faithful servant'?"

Here we find the first key to surviving the ungodly locker room environment: making a conscious choice to follow Christ.

Taking a stand brings us to requirement number two: guts.

"You have to have some kind of stability and the ability to stand strong," said pitcher Andy Pettitte of the New York Yankees. "If you stand fast, God's going to be faithful; He's going to bless you."

The Lord provides several tools that equip and strengthen us for the task. The first is the Bible.

"Just like we feed our bodies physically with food and water we have to feed our spirits with the Word of God," said Luke Scott, also with the Baltimore Orioles.

**ANOTHER TOOL WE ARE GIVEN IS THE ACCOUNTABILITY OF FELLOW BELIEVERS.**

"Having teammates who share my faith is great because we support and encourage each other," Scott said. "It may be OK to go hang out with your friends and joke and have a good time, but there are guidelines and certain barriers that we don't cross. As Christians, we understand that we're to be set apart. For me, I go hang out with my teammates, but there are certain topics I don't joke about or certain beliefs I won't agree with, and that's fine. I stick up for what I believe in, and that in and of itself is a witness."

From FCA's *Sharing the Victory* magazine

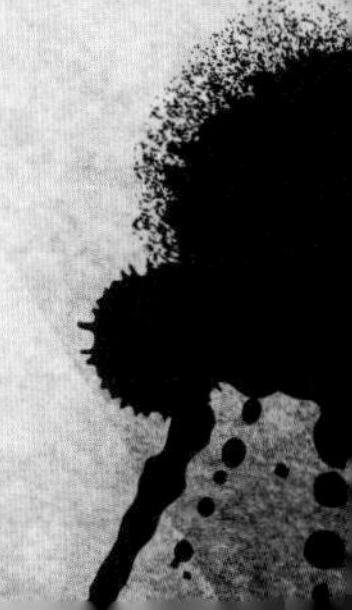

"As for me and my family, we will worship the LORD" (Joshua 24:15). What are some areas in your life where you can set a better example and show others that, like Joshua, you "will worship the Lord"?

BLAH BLAH BLAH

☐ BLAH

BLAH BLAH BLAH

☐ BLAH

BLAH BLAH BLAH

☐ BLAH

Just like the foundation for a gamechanging sports team starts in the draft room, your successful life as a believer starts as you "draft" teammates to join you in the good fight. Recruit new teammates who share the same beliefs, values, and goals, and are willing to keep you accountable in your Christian walk.

**A man with many friends may be harmed, but there is a friend who stays closer than a brother.** — Proverbs 18:24

**Make a list of outstanding gamechanging characteristics you value. List three people you know who possess these characteristics. Make a commitment to seek out these people. If you can't think of anyone you know with these characteristics, ask God to put new friends in your life who exhibit those traits.**

**Iron sharpens iron, and one man sharpens another.... As the water reflects the face, so the heart reflects the person.** — Proverbs 27:17, 19

**As we allow God to form a gamechanging team around us, we will be better equipped to face life's challenges and more effective as we reach out to others with His gospel of love and redemption.**

**A friend loves at all times, and a brother is born for a difficult time.**
— Proverbs 17:17

## MASTERING THE GAME
BY CLAY MEYER

PGA TOUR PRO ZACH JOHNSON IS A SELF-PROCLAIMED SPORTS ENTHUSIAST. AND, AS A CHRISTIAN, HE READILY ADMITS THAT HIS FAVORITE STORY IS ONE WHERE SPORTS AND SCRIPTURE COLLIDE: DAVID VERSUS GOLIATH. AT THE MERE MENTION OF THE BIBLICAL BATTLE, JOHNSON SEES FLASHES OF A SMALL SHEPHERD BOY WITH A SLING AND STONES OVERTAKING A PHILISTINE GIANT. IMMEDIATELY HE IS INSPIRED.

The fact that Johnson loves this story shouldn't come as a surprise considering he was the sports edition of David when he won the Masters in 2007. He'd walked the plush greens of Augusta National Golf Club as an obscure Midwesterner in only his third year on the PGA Tour and defeated the giants of the game. And like David, Johnson knew he wasn't overcoming the odds alone. He was competing in the strength of his heavenly Father and knew that, if he was meant to win the biggest tournament in professional golf, it would be for the sole purpose of giving God the glory.

That Easter Sunday, after tapping in a final putt that put him two strokes ahead of the field and eventually secured his title, Johnson was greeted by his wife, Kim, and 3-month-old son, Will, in an emotional embrace that he still struggles to describe. When the final

pairings finished, each player coming up just shy of Johnson's score, it became official: Zach Johnson was the Master's champion.

On this career-defining day, just after he walked off the course, Johnson told the national television audience what the victory really meant.

**"MY CHRISTIAN FAITH IS VERY IMPORTANT TO ME," HE SAID. "IT WAS VERY SPECIAL TO WIN THE MASTERS GOLF TOURNAMENT ON EASTER SUNDAY. I'M VERY BLESSED. I WOULD LIKE TO THANK GOD. I FELT JESUS CHRIST WITH ME ON THE GOLF COURSE EVERY STEP OF THE WAY."**

The humble Midwesterner had done the unthinkable and slayed the giants of golf. And, following the example David set years ago, he directed the praise and honor to his heavenly Father.

From FCA's *Sharing the Victory* magazine

**What makes a man is the ability to sacrificially give expecting nothing in return, and what makes a leader is someone who is willing to die to self every day for the benefit of the team.** — Heath Evans

**No one has greater love than this, that someone would lay down his life for his friends.** — John 15:13

**What are some ways you have made yourself available for whatever the coach needed from you? Now thinking of God as your Coach, tell how you can make yourself available to Him.**

**Then I heard the voice of the Lord saying: Who should I send? Who will go for Us? I said: Here I am. Send me.** — Isaiah 6:8

In the world of sports, the gamechanger is usually considered an athlete who steps up and makes a key play that helps his or her team bring home the big win. In God's kingdom, the ultimate gamechanger is someone who recognizes the needs of others and reaches out to help by showing them the love of Christ.

**For Christ's love compels us, since we have reached this conclusion: if One died for all, then all died. And He died for all so that those who live should no longer live for themselves, but for the One who died for them and was raised.** — 2 Corinthians 5:14–15

**There is no greater fulfillment in life than to share the love of Christ and His message of hope and salvation with others in your world. As you trust God to equip you and use you for His purpose, you will finally understand the truth behind what it means to be a gamechanger.**

**All authority has been given to Me in heaven and on earth. Go, therefore, and make disciples of all nations...teaching them to observe everything I have commanded you. And remember, I am with you always, to the end of the age.**
— Matthew 28:18–20

**When an athlete receives his or her self-worth from God, it frees the athlete to play for an audience of One. When God is your audience, you can find joy in all circumstances.**

**Whatever you do, work at it with all your heart, as working for the Lord, not for men, since you know that you will receive an inheritance from the Lord as a reward. It is the Lord Christ you are serving.** — Colossians 3:23–24 NIV

**God doesn't call the equipped, He equips the called. In other words, God will give you everything you need to be a gamechanger in someone else's life.**

**Do not fear, for I am with you; do not be afraid, for I am your God. I will strengthen you; I will help you; I will hold on to you with My righteous right hand.** — Isaiah 41:10

## THE SOUL SURFER
BY JOSHUA COOLEY

BETHANY HAMILTON'S FIRST THIRTEEN YEARS WERE LIKE A POSTCARD—IDYLLIC AND PICTURESQUE. ON HER HAWAIIAN ISLAND HOME HER PARENTS RAISED HER AND HER TWO OLDER BROTHERS TO LOVE GOD AND SURFING.

She placed her faith in Christ at age five and became quite active in her youth group at North Shore Christian Fellowship Church in Kilauea, Kauai. She climbed on her first surfboard as a toddler. By age seven, she could catch a wave without help, and by thirteen she placed second at the National Scholastic Surfing Association (NSSA) national championships. A new surf queen was emerging—one who could show the world the love of Christ through the power of a surfboard.

Then came Halloween.

On October 31, 2003, Hamilton was surfing her home breaks on Kauai's North Shore. She was lying flat on her board when it happened. A fourteen-foot tiger shark severed her arm and took a huge chunk out of her board.

At the hospital, Hamilton underwent several successful surgeries. She lost her arm just below the shoulder, but her life had been spared.

While others might have been too afraid to return to the ocean after a traumatic experience like that, Hamilton wasn't. She returned to the water just three weeks later and quickly learned how to surf one-armed with the help of custom-made boards. Then, a mere three months after the attack, she placed fifth in the open women's division of an NSSA competition on Oahu. Now a full-time pro, Hamilton competed in more than ten events last year.

**"IN EARLY OCTOBER 2003, MY MOM AND I STARTED PRAYING AND ASKING GOD TO USE ME AND SHOW ME HIS PURPOSE FOR MY LIFE," HAMILTON SAID. "SO, AFTER THE SHARK ATTACK, I ACCEPTED THAT GOD ALLOWED THIS TO HAPPEN TO ME FOR A REASON."**

"It's truly humbling, but a blessing to have been given a platform to share my faith. God just opened up the door for me to talk about His love to people all around the world rather than what would have otherwise been just the surfing community. It's pretty cool."

From FCA's *Sharing the Victory* magazine

**Christ didn't come just to make us better people. He came to die for us and to let us know that He was the better person. I want people to know that everything good in me comes from Him and not my own effort.** — Ben Zobrist

**Those who are wise will shine like the brightness of the heavens, and those who lead many to righteousness, like the stars for ever and ever.**
— Daniel 12:3 NIV

**Just because I am away from home doesn't mean Jesus isn't with me. He is everywhere, and you can see signs of Him in the most remote places in the world through people who don't even speak your language. Jesus is universal.** — DeLisha Milton-Jones

**Everything has a purpose: the school you attend, the home you live in, the team on which you play, and so on. Nothing is an accident in God's eyes.**

**We know that all things work together for the good of those who love God: those who are called according to His purpose.** — Romans 8:28

God has you at this specific place, at this specific time, for His specific purpose. Looking at where you are in life right now—in your home, on your team, and at your school—what do you think God might be calling you to do?

**I will instruct you and show you the way to go; with My eye on you, I will give counsel.** — Psalm 32:8

# RAY OF LIGHT: TAMPA BAY ALL-STAR BEN ZOBRIST
BY JILL EWERT

BEN ZOBRIST THOUGHT HIS BASEBALL DAYS WERE OVER WHEN HE FINISHED HIS SENIOR SEASON AT EUREKA HIGH SCHOOL IN EUREKA, ILL.

"I did a lot of questioning that year and trying to figure out where I was going in life," said Zobrist. "I had a lot of anxiety that I had to release to the Lord. And that's when everything started opening up."

At the end of June, Zobrist participated in a nearby skills showcase for coaches and scouts. One of the coaches on hand was NAIA legend Elliot Johnson from Olivet Nazarene University (Ill.). In the young Zobrist, Johnson saw potential no one else did. He offered Zobrist a place on the team.

As a pitcher and infielder at Olivet, Zobrist developed his skills on the field but impressed others by investing equal if not greater effort into his spiritual growth. He led the campus FCA Huddle and contributed to the team's spiritual development.

After a quality career with the Tigers, Zobrist prayed about and made the decision to transfer to Division-I Dallas Baptist University for his senior year. It was a God-ordained, prayed-up decision that paid off, as Zobrist was noticed and selected by the Houston Astros in the 2004 MLB Draft.

Midway through the 2006 season, the Astros traded him to the Tampa Bay Rays. He endured two up-and-down years but altered his swing prior to the start of the 2008 season and returned to the team with a powerful bat. Zobrist continued his individual success in 2009. And as his on-the-field stock has risen, so has his fame.

**"I FEEL REALLY HUMBLED BY THE FACT THAT I HAVE A PLATFORM," SAID ZOBRIST.**

"What God has taught me over the years as He's kept me in the game is that ministry can happen anywhere—wherever we work; wherever we go—but it has to happen in our own hearts first. Then, He will take our lives and connect them to those around us. It doesn't matter if it's a baseball field, a clubhouse, a backyard or a neighborhood. Wherever we go, we will be His vessels."

From FCA's *Sharing the Victory* magazine

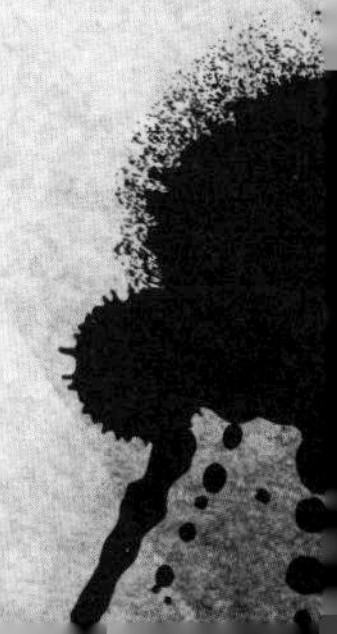

**The key to being a gamechanger for Christ has nothing to do with our talent or ability, but rather our availability. It's about putting yourself in a position to be used by God, and then trusting that He will give you the words to say and the boldness to say them.**

**But the LORD said to me, “Do not say, ‘I am only a child.’ You must go to everyone I send you to and say whatever I command you. Do not be afraid of them, for I am with you and will rescue you,” declares the LORD. Then the LORD reached out his hand and touched my mouth and said to me, “Now, I have put my words in your mouth.”** — Jeremiah 1:7–9 NIV

**If you will commit to surround yourself with godly influencers and give Jesus Christ control over 100 percent of your life, the end result will be the same as the new believers experienced in Acts 2:47: "And every day the Lord added to them those who were being saved." You will change your world.**

Ellie Claire™ Gift & Paper Corp.
Minneapolis, MN 55438
www.ellieclaire.com

**Gamechanger: Make a Play**
Athletes' Journal



ISBN 978-1-60936-200-3



Compiled by Jill Jones
Cover and interior design by Studio Gear Box | studiogearbox.com

Printed in China.

GAME
CHANGER

GAME
CHANGER